Let's Talk About Being Afraid

Anna Kreiner

The Rosen Publishing Group's
PowerKids Press™
New York

Published in 1996 by The Rosen Publishing Group, Inc.
29 East 21st Street, New York, NY 10010

First Edition

Photo credits: Cover photo © Ken Horii/International Stock; p. 4 © George Ancona/International Stock; p. 7 © Chuck Mason/International Stock; p. 8 © Stan Pak/International Stock; pp. 11, 12 © Scott Thode/International Stock; pp. 15, 20 © John Michael/International Stock; p. 16 © Jeff Greenberg/International Stock; p. 19 © Chad Ehlers/International Stock.

Book Design and Layout: Erin McKenna

Kreiner, Anna.
    Let's talk about being afraid / Anna Kreiner. — 1st ed.
        p.   cm. — (The let's talk library)
    Includes index.
    Summary: A simple introduction to what causes fear and how to handle being afraid.
    ISBN 0-8239-2305-3
    1. Fear in children. [1. Fear.] I. Title. II. Series
BF723.F4K73   1996
155.4'1246—dc20   96-48382
                                         CIP
                                          AC

Manufactured in the United States of America

Table of Contents

What Are You Afraid Of?

Are you afraid of the dark? Do ghost stories give you scary dreams? Are you afraid to go into the basement or the attic? Do insects give you the creepy-crawlies? Are you afraid when your parents fight?

Everyone feels afraid sometimes, even grown-ups. When you feel afraid, you worry that something bad will happen to you or to someone that you know or love.

◀ People are afraid of lots of things, such as insects.

Fear

Being afraid means feeling fear. Fear is an **emotion** (ee-MOE-shun). Happiness, sadness, and anger are other emotions. Everyone feels these emotions sometimes. Even your mom or dad.

Fear is not a bad emotion. It can help keep you safe. But too much fear can be harmful. It can keep you from doing fun things, like making new friends, or things that are good for you, like going to the doctor.

Telling an adult that you're afraid can help you get over your fears. ▶

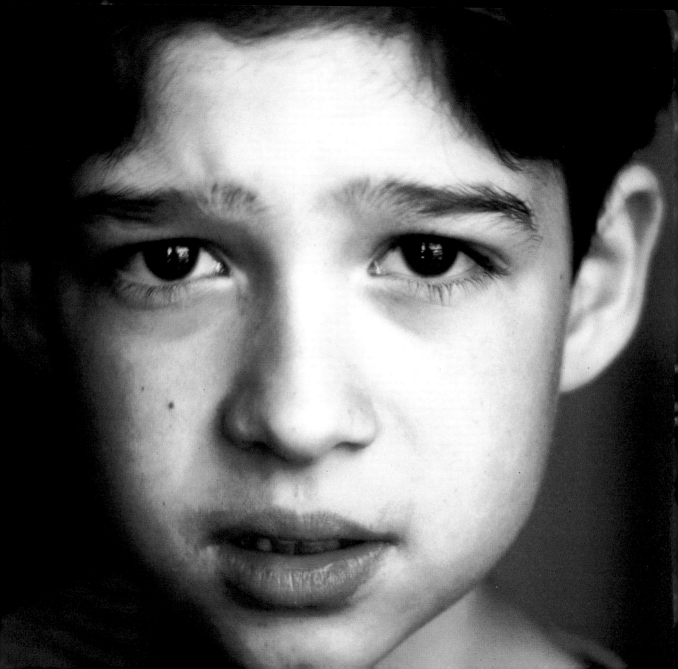

Knowing When You Are Afraid

Your body usually tells you when you are afraid. Your heart begins to beat faster. It may be hard to swallow. You may feel "butterflies" in your stomach. This is because your body is preparing you to fight or run away from what you are afraid of. This is normal. This is how your body protects you.

The way to make your body feel better is to make the fear go away.

◀ Your body lets you know
when you're afraid.

9

Why Are You Afraid?

Sometimes you know why you're afraid. Maybe you were bitten by a dog, and now you're scared of dogs. You may have seen a scary show about a clown, and now you don't like clowns. It's okay to be afraid of these kinds of things.

Other times you may not know why you are afraid. You may not know why thunder scares you. Or why a certain person scares you. It's okay to be afraid of these kinds of things too.

Lots of people think clowns are scary. ▶

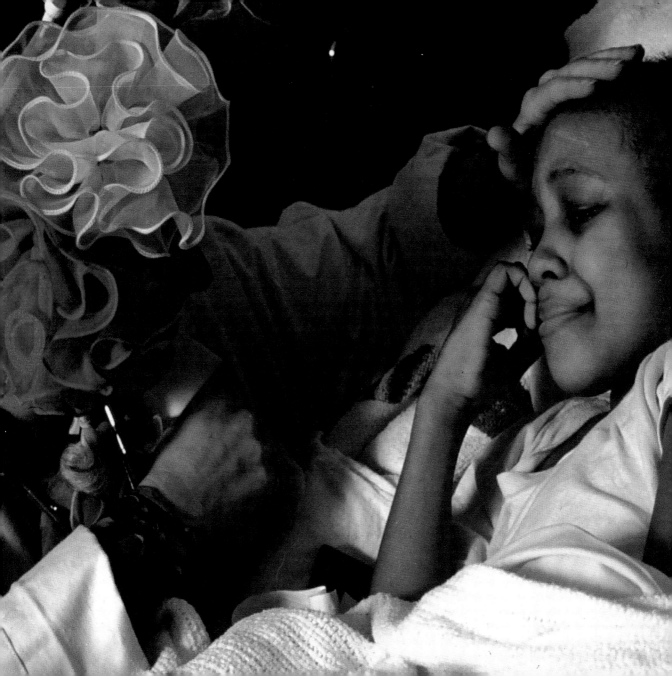

Special Kinds of Fear

Really strong feelings of fear are called **phobias** (FOE-bee-yas). Someone who is scared of heights has **acrophobia** (AK-roe-FOE-bee-ya). Someone who is afraid of being in a small space has **claustrophobia** (KLOS-tro-FOE-bee-ya). Some people live their whole lives being afraid of heights or small spaces.

You probably don't have a phobia. But you may have a fear. And there are things you can do to help make it go away.

◀ You probably don't have acrophobia, but you may sometimes be afraid of heights.

Things That Have Hurt You

Sometimes you are afraid of things that have hurt you, like dogs or a hot stove or a bully. These fears are good. They keep you from getting hurt again. If you are afraid of getting burned, you won't touch a hot stove. But knowing that these fears are good doesn't make feeling the fears any easier. Tell your parents, a teacher, or a good friend how you're feeling. Just knowing that somebody else knows and cares can help make the fear go away.

Telling your dad how you feel ▶
may make you feel better.

Imaginary Creatures

You may be afraid of **imaginary** (im-MAJ-in-air-ee) creatures like monsters or bad fairies or ghosts. Here are two ways to deal with these fears.

- Try to understand that these creatures can't hurt you because they can't touch you. They only exist when you read books or tell stories about them.
- Tell the story to yourself. Only change it so that the scary monster is actually a friendly monster who helps you.

◀ Your brother or sister may be able to help you change the story so it's not as scary.

New Things

You may be afraid of new situations, such as moving to a new school or neighborhood. You may be afraid that you won't make friends or that you'll get lost in your new building. The way to get rid of these fears is to prepare for the new situation. Ask your parents to take you to meet your new teacher. See if there are any other kids in your new neighborhood or building. Doing something to prepare yourself will help make the fears go away.

Ask your mom to show you your new neighborhood. ▶

Things You Can't Change

You may have heard about a war on TV. Or your neighbor's house was broken into. Or someone you know was hurt. You may be afraid that one of these things may happen to you or someone you love.

Tell your parents or a teacher how you feel. They may not be able to prevent these things from happening. But they can help keep you as safe as possible. Knowing that they understand may make you feel better.

◀ Your parents want to keep you safe and happy.

It's Okay to Be Afraid

It's okay to be scared. Everyone is afraid sometimes. You can't always make your fears go away. But you can take care of yourself by talking to other people about your fears. Who knows? You may find that someone else has the same fears that you do. You can help each other by talking about them.

Glossary

acrophobia (AK-roe-FOE-bee-ya) Strong fear of heights.

claustrophobia (KLOS-tro-FOE-bee-ya) Strong fear of being in small spaces.

emotion (ee-MOE-shun) A feeling.

imaginary (im-MAJ-in-air-ee) Something that isn't real.

phobia (FOE-bee-ya) A strong fear.

Index